DO YOU WANT A PET CHINCHILLA?

BY LOUIS MALLORY

Enslow PUBLISHING

THAT'S AN ODD PET!

Please visit our website, www.enslow.com. For a free color catalog of all our high-quality books, call toll free 1-800-398-2504 or fax 1-877-980-4454.

Library of Congress Cataloging-in-Publication Data

Names: Mallory, Louis, author.
Title: Do your want a pet chinchilla? / Louis Mallory.
Description: Buffalo, NY : Enslow Publishing, [2025] | Series: That's an odd pet! | Includes index.
Identifiers: LCCN 2023054284 (print) | LCCN 2023054285 (ebook) | ISBN 9781978540750 (library binding) | ISBN 9781978540743 (paperback) | ISBN 9781978540767 (ebook)
Subjects: LCSH: Chinchillas as pets–Juvenile literature.
Classification: LCC SF459.C48 M35 2025 (print) | LCC SF459.C48 (ebook) | DDC 636.935/93–dc23/eng/20240102
LC record available at https://lccn.loc.gov/2023054284
LC ebook record available at https://lccn.loc.gov/2023054285

Published in 2025 by
Enslow Publishing
2544 Clinton Street
Buffalo, NY 14224

Copyright © 2025 Enslow Publishing

Portions of this work were originally authored by Grace Houser and published as *Chinchillas*. All new material in this edition is authored by Louis Mallory.

Designer: Claire Zimmermann
Editor: Natalie Humphrey

Photo credits: Cover (photo) Patrycja Skworc/Shutterstock.com; Series Art (title and heading font, texture) Gleb Guralnyk/Shutterstock.com; Series Art (background retro swirl) ChekmanDaria/Shutterstock.com; Series Art (corner dots) Romanova Ekaterina/Shutterstock.com; Series Art (body text boxes, page number background shape) Angie Makes/Shutterstock.com; Series Art (hand-drawn doodles) yugoro/Shutterstock.com; pp. 5, 15, 19 Irina Vasilevskaia/Shutterstock.com; pp. 7, 17 Luniaka Maria/Shutterstock.com; p. 9 meunierd/Shutterstock.com; p. 11 icealien/Shutterstock.com; p. 13 kesterhu/Shutterstock.com.

All rights reserved. No part of this book may be reproduced in any form without permission in writing from the publisher, except by a reviewer.

Some of the images in this book illustrate individuals who are models. The depictions do not imply actual situations or events.

Printed in the United States of America

CPSIA compliance information: Batch #CSENS25: For further information contact Enslow Publishing at 1-800-398-2504.

CONTENTS

Fuzzy Friends 4
Big Rodents 6
Wild Chinchillas 8
Getting Your Pet Chinchilla 10
Chinchilla Cages 12
Your Chinchilla's Dinner 14
Taking Care of Your Chinchilla 16
Dusty Baths 18
Holding Your Pet 20
Glossary 22
For More Information 23
Index 24

Words in the glossary appear in **bold** type the first time they are used in the text.

FUZZY FRIENDS

You might not have heard of this odd ball of fur before, but there's a lot to love about chinchillas! This little animal has one of the thickest coats around. This **dense** fur makes it very soft to the touch.

JUST THE FACTS!

Chinchillas can usually live up to about 10 years in the wild. With the right care, though, chinchillas can live for 20 years.

Chinchillas are social animals that need a lot of love and attention.

If you're looking for a cuddly pet small enough to hold in your arms, a chinchilla might be perfect for you. But before you run out and buy your own furry friend, make sure you know how to take care of your new pet.

BIG RODENTS

Chinchillas are **rodents**. They have large, round ears that they use to listen for danger and to keep themselves cool when it's hot. Adult chinchillas are usually 9 to 14 inches (23 to 35 cm) long and can weigh up to about 1.8 pounds (0.8 kg). They also have a long tail that helps them balance.

Chinchillas **shed** year-round. Chinchillas can usually take care of their own coats. But you can brush your chinchilla if it needs help.

Chinchilla fur can be gray, black, white, silver, tan, or somewhat blue!

JUST THE FACTS!

Chinchilla fur is thick and soft, but doesn't usually bother people's **allergies**. If you're allergic to cats and dogs, a chinchilla may make a better pet for you.

WILD CHINCHILLAS

Wild chinchillas can be found in South America. They live high up in the Andes Mountains where it can be quite cold. The cold weather isn't a problem for chinchillas, though. Their thick fur helps to keep them warm.

JUST THE FACTS!

The long-tailed chinchilla is most common to have as a pet.

Chinchillas can be found hiding in spaces between rocks or digging tunnels **underground**.

There are two **species** of chinchillas: long-tailed and short-tailed. They live in large groups called herds. These herds can have over 100 chinchillas! Chinchillas are **endangered** in the wild.

Getting Your Pet Chinchilla

If you decide to get a pet chinchilla, you can adopt one from an **animal shelter** or buy one from a pet store. Chinchillas aren't easy pets to keep though. They need a lot of attention. Make sure you have the time to care for one.

Just the Facts!

A nervous chinchilla might try to bite. Chinchilla bites can be painful and even bleed.

Never grab your chinchilla by the tail!

Chinchillas have lots of **energy** and can be a little nervous. They're not good pets for very young children. An energetic child might frighten or hurt a pet chinchilla by mistake.

CHINCHILLA CAGES

Chinchillas need special cages. Their cage needs to be big enough for them to run and jump. A large wire cage is the perfect home. The floor of your cage shouldn't be wired because it may hurt your pet's paws.

JUST THE FACTS!

Chinchillas can jump up to 6 feet (1.8 m) in the air!

You can cover the bottom of your chinchilla's cage with **fabric** to help protect its paws.

You can put bedding made of fleece fabric in your pet chinchilla's cage. Don't use pine or cedar wood for bedding as it can be sharp. Give your pet places to rest and hide, such as a box or tube.

YOUR CHINCHILLA'S DINNER

Chinchillas eat mostly hay. Hay should always be left in your chinchilla's cage so it can eat whenever it's hungry. Chinchillas should be given some special food **pellets** too. Chinchillas should also always have fresh, clean water. Check on your chinchilla throughout the day to make sure it has enough food and clean water.

Chinchillas can be given some dried fruit or apple wood sticks as treats. These foods shouldn't be given to your chinchilla too often though.

When a chinchilla eats, it holds its food in its front paws.

JUST THE FACTS!

A chinchillas will sometimes eat its own poop! This is called coprophagy and while it looks gross, it helps the chinchilla get more **nutrients** from its food.

Taking Care of Your Chinchilla

Keeping your chinchilla healthy is important. Sometimes, these little critters get sick or hurt. If your chinchilla isn't eating or drinking, seems less active than usual, or is having trouble breathing, you should take your pet to the vet for a checkup.

Chinchillas may overheat if it's more than 75°F (24°C) where they're kept. If your chinchilla gets too hot, you can help it cool down with cool water.

If your chinchilla's teeth are too long, a vet can cut them to help your chinchilla eat.

JUST THE FACTS!

Just like other rodents, a chinchilla's teeth never stop growing. Make sure to give your chinchilla hay and safe wooden sticks or chew toys to help keep their teeth from getting too long.

DUSTY BATHS

To keep your chinchilla clean, never give it baths in water. Because a chinchilla's fur is so thick, it has a tough time drying off when it's wet. Chinchillas take baths in dust instead! Rolling around in dust helps them get rid of extra oil on their fur.

JUST THE FACTS!

Chinchillas are naturally clean animals, but you can help them stay clean! Be sure to change the bedding in your chinchilla's cage once a week or more if needed.

A healthy chinchilla shouldn't have a strong smell.

You can buy your chinchilla bath dust from a pet store. Twice a week, put some dust in a large bowl. Place your chinchilla in the bowl and let it roll around to clean itself.

HOLDING YOUR PET

Chinchillas are happiest when they're in pairs. If you can only have one chinchilla, make sure you give it lots of attention and play with it often.

If you pick up your chinchilla, be gentle and use both hands! Keep your pet close to your body. You may want to sit down or stay close to the ground when you hold your chinchilla. That way it won't get hurt if it jumps or gets away from you.

TAKING CARE OF YOUR CHINCHILLA!

- Make sure your chinchilla has plenty of hay to eat throughout the day.
- Give your chinchilla toys it can safely chew on.
- Be sure your chinchilla gets a lot of exercise.
- Make sure your chinchilla doesn't get too hot!
- Give your chinchilla a dust bath twice a week.
- Spend a lot of time with your chinchilla, but be sure to be careful if you hold it!

JUST THE FACTS!

Chinchillas have long leg bones that can break easily. Hold your chinchilla gently and make sure to never squish it.

GLOSSARY

allergy: A body's sensitivity to usually harmless things in surroundings, such as dust, pollen, or mold.

animal shelter: A place where people take lost animals or animals without an owner.

dense: Packed very closely together.

endangered: In danger of dying out.

energy: The ability to be active.

fabric: A kind of cloth.

nutrient: Something a living thing needs to grow and stay alive.

pellet: A small piece of animal food.

rodent: A small, furry animal with large front teeth, such as a mouse or rat.

shed: To lose fur.

species: A group of plants or animals that are all the same kind.

underground: Beneath the ground's surface.

For More Information

Books

Lowe, Lindsey. *Rodents*. Tucson, AZ: Brown Bear Books, 2023.

Marcos, Victoria. *Chinchillas*. Rosenberg, TX: Xist Publishing, 2021.

Websites

Britannica Kids: Chinchilla
kids.britannica.com/students/article/chinchilla/273640
Learn more about chinchillas in the wild.

Critter Squad: Chinchilla
www.crittersquad.com/fact-sheets/chinchilla-fact-sheet/
Learn more facts about chinchillas.

Publisher's note to educators and parents: Our editors have carefully reviewed these websites to ensure that they are suitable for students. Many websites change frequently, however, and we cannot guarantee that a site's future contents will continue to meet our high standards of quality and educational value. Be advised that students should be closely supervised whenever they access the internet.

Index

attention, 5, 10, 20
bedding, 13, 18
bite, 10
bones, 21
coat, 4, 6
dust, 18, 19, 21
ears, 6
food, 14, 15
fur, 4, 7, 8, 18
groups, 9
jumping, 12, 20
life span, 4
long-tailed chinchilla, 8, 9

overheating, 16
paws, 12, 13, 15
poop, 15
short-tailed chinchilla, 9
size, 6
smell, 19
South America, 8
tail, 6, 9, 11
teeth, 17
vet, 16, 17
water, 14, 16, 18
weather, 8